The Science of Light & Color

LIVING SCIENCE

Patricia Miller-Schroeder

Gareth Stevens Publishing
A WORLD ALMANAC EDUCATION GROUP COMPANY

For a free color catalog describing Gareth Stevens' list of high-quality books and multimedia programs, call 1-800-542-2595 (USA) or 1-800-461-9120 (Canada). Gareth Stevens Publishing's Fax: (414) 225-0377.

Library of Congress Cataloging-in-Publication Data available upon request from publisher. Fax (414) 225-0377 for the attention of the Publishing Records Department.

ISBN 1-8368-2679-5 (lib. bdg.)

This edition first published in 2000 by
Gareth Stevens Publishing
A World Almanac Education Group Company
1555 North RiverCenter Drive, Suite 201
Milwaukee, WI 53212 USA

Project Co-ordinator: Rennay Craats
Series Editor: Celeste Peters
Copy Editors: Heather Kissock and Megan Lappi
Design: Warren Clark
Cover Design: Lucinda Cage and Terry Paulhus
Layout: Lucinda Cage
Gareth Stevens Editor: Patricia Lantier-Sampon

Every reasonable effort has been made to trace ownership and to obtain permission to reprint copyright material. The publishers would be pleased to have any errors or omissions brought to their attention so that they may be corrected in subsequent printings.

Photograph Credits:
American Optical Corporation: page 21 bottom right. Corel Corporation: cover (center), pages 4, 5 left, 5 right, 5 bottom, 6 top, 6 bottom, 7 bottom, 9, 12, 15 top, 17, 20 top, 20 bottom left, 21 top, 21 bottom, 22 left, 23 top, 23 bottom, 24 top, 24 bottom, 25 bottom left, 25 bottom right, 29. Corbis: cover (background). Digital Stock: page 22 bottom. EyeWire: pages 16, 22 top right, 27 bottom right. Doranne Jacobson: pages 7 top, 14. Roy McLean: pages 10 top, 10 bottom, 27 top left. Tom Stack & Associates: pages 25 top (Jeff Foott), 26 (Spencer Swanger), 28 top (Kitchin & Hurst), 28 bottom (Joe McDonald). Visuals Unlimited: pages 11 (Mark E. Gibson), 13 (Jeff J. Daly), 15 bottom (Cheyenne Rouse), 18 top (Arthur Hill), 18 bottom (Mundy Hackett).

Printed in Canada

1 2 3 4 5 6 7 8 9 04 03 02 01 00

Contents

What Do You Know about
Light and Color?. 4

A Splash of Color 6

Colors of Light 8

Light and Shadow 10

   Rainbows and Prisms 12

   Colors of Paints and Dyes. 14

Polka Dot Pictures 16

Seeing Light and Color. 18

Red and Green Cannot Be Seen 20

Plants and Light 22

Hiding in Color. 24

Focus on Photographers 26

Warning Colors 28

Color Safari 30

Glossary 32

Index 32

Web Sites 32

What Do You Know about Light and Color?

O ur world is full of light and color. The colors of a rainbow, your shadow on the sidewalk, and the pictures on a television screen all come from light. Light contains color. Color gives us information about the world around us. It tells us when food is ready to eat. Color also gives us messages about danger. It can attract attention or even make things seem to disappear.

Without light from the Sun, most life on Earth could not exist. Plants need light to live and grow. In turn, plants provide food and **oxygen** for animals and people. Without light, Earth would be a dull and lifeless place.

Male peacocks strut for females. They show off their bright feathers by fanning them out.

Activity

How Many Colors Can You Find?

Have a friend time you while you make a list of all the colors you can see in five minutes. Switch places and time your friend. Compare lists. Which colors are the most common?

Some people wear colorful jewelry to make their clothing more exciting.

Some animals, such as owls, use protective coloring to hide from other animals.

A Splash of Color

P eople have used light and color for thousands of years. Light and color make their homes attractive and comfortable. People also use light and color to express themselves through their clothing, home decoration, and art.

Light and color are important in many celebrations. Christmas, for example, calls for candles, tree lights, and red and green colors.

During the Hindu festival of Holi, people throw colored water over each other. This shows the return of color and warmth to the land in spring.

Light and color can make people feel certain ways. Long nights and less sunshine in winter make some people feel sad. Most people say they feel happier and more alert in well-lit places. Walls painted with soft, soothing colors, like pale green or blue, can make people feel more relaxed.

Colors can show that people belong to certain groups. These soldiers' blue hats show they are with the United Nations.

Puzzler

What do you think the following sayings mean?
a. good as gold
b. feeling blue
c. seeing red
d. feeling off-color

Answer:
a. very good or worth a lot
b. feeling sad
c. feeling angry
d. not feeling well or like oneself.

Colors of Light

The white light we see from the Sun contains many colors. These include the three **primary colors** of light — red, blue, and green. All the other colors are made by mixing these three colors. Light looks white when it contains all three primary colors. When there is no light, there is no color, and black is the result.

Sunlight shines through a **transparent** object such as glass. If the transparent object is colored, it lets only light of the same color pass through. For example, red glass lets only red light shine through. The glass **absorbs** all the other colors.

The Colors of Light

Black	Red	Magenta	Blue	Cyan
• no light present • no color	• a primary color of light	• reddish-purple • a mixture of red and blue • green is absent	• a primary color of light	• bluish-green • a mixture of green and blue • red is absent

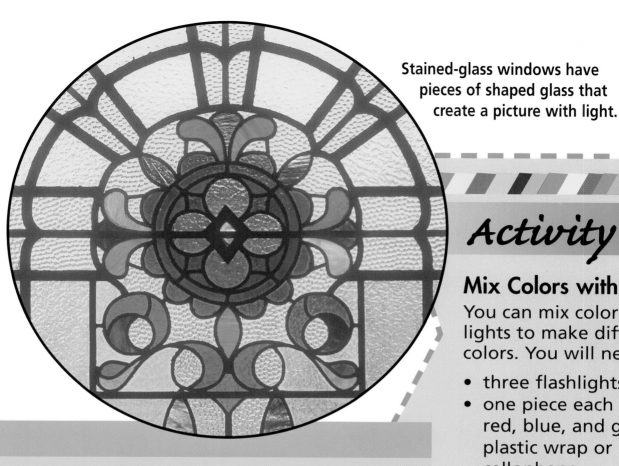

Stained-glass windows have pieces of shaped glass that create a picture with light.

Green	Yellow	White
• a primary color of light	• a mixture of red and green • blue is absent	• a mixture of the primary colors red, blue, and green

Activity

Mix Colors with Light

You can mix colored lights to make different colors. You will need:

- three flashlights
- one piece each of red, blue, and green plastic wrap or cellophane
- a large piece of white paper or a white wall

1. Put one piece of plastic wrap or cellophane over the end of each flashlight.
2. Shine the flashlights onto the white paper or wall.
3. Overlap the colors. What other colors are created?

Light and Shadow

When light hits an object and cannot shine through it, a shadow forms. A shadow is a dark area behind the object where light cannot reach. The shadow shows the outline of the object that is blocking the light.

People can create different shapes with their shadows. Hand shadows are used to perform puppet plays against screens or white walls.

All solid objects, including people, buildings, and animals, cast shadows.

Materials that block light are **opaque**. Many solid objects, including wood, stone, cloth, paper, plastic, bone, and metal, are opaque. You cast a shadow because your body is opaque.

The size of the shadow you cast gets smaller as you move away from an object that gives off light. For example, when you are near a light bulb, you cast a big shadow on the wall. If you step away from the light bulb, you block less light. Your shadow is smaller.

Activity

Shadow Drawings

Make face shadow drawings with a friend.

1. Tape a sheet of paper on a wall.
2. Sit on a chair in front of the paper with your head turned to one side.
3. Dim the room light and shine a flashlight on one side of your face. Be sure not to look directly at the light. A shadow of your face will appear on the paper.
4. Have a friend draw around the face shadow on the paper.
5. Then change places and draw your friend's shadow.

Shadows fall on the side of the object opposite the light source. If the Sun is behind you, the shadow falls in front of you.

Rainbows and Prisms

Sunlight travels through the air in a straight line. If it enters another substance, such as water or glass, it changes direction slightly. It bends. This bending is called **refraction**. Different colors of light bend more than others. Red light bends the least, and violet light bends the most.

A rainbow forms when sunlight shines through water droplets in the air. Sunlight bends when it passes through water droplets. The bent sunlight forms an arch showing all the colors of light. The colors of a rainbow are red, orange, yellow, green, blue, and violet.

An old legend says there is a pot of gold at the end of a rainbow.

Sunlight also spreads out into colors when it shines through a glass object called a **prism**. A prism bends light into its rainbow colors. Prisms can be used in binoculars to **reflect** light and help people see long distances.

As light enters a prism, it bends. The bending separates the light into different colors.

Puzzler

Rainbows often form after rain showers. Can they form any other time?

Answer:
Rainbows can form whenever there are water droplets in the air. Often you can find a rainbow in the spray of a waterfall or a garden sprinkler.

Colors of Paints and Dyes

Paints and dyes get their color from substances called **pigments**. The primary colors of pigment are different from the primary colors of light. Primary pigment colors are red, blue, and yellow. Mixing these three colors makes black. In contrast, mixing red, blue, and green, the primary colors of light, makes white.

A color wheel is a display of colors as they relate to each other. It shows how pigment colors mix to form other colors.

Paint contains pigment colors. Pigments mix to form many additional colors.

Pigment color is the color that reflects, or bounces, off an object. This is the color you see. The object absorbs all other colors. For example, a flower with yellow pigment reflects only yellow light to your eyes. The flower absorbs all the other colors of light. Grass reflects the color green and absorbs other colors.

A white object reflects all the colors of light. A black object does not reflect any light at all.

Puzzler

Think of an orange fruit. What colors of light reflect from its surface?

Answer:
Red and yellow light reflect from the surface of the fruit. These two colors combine to make the color orange.

Polka Dot Pictures

Tiny dots of color create the pictures on your television. Groups of blue, red, and green dots cover the inside of the screen. Different patterns of these dots light up. This light combines to make all the colors you see on the television. For example, where only red dots light up, you see red. Where red and green dots light up, you see yellow.

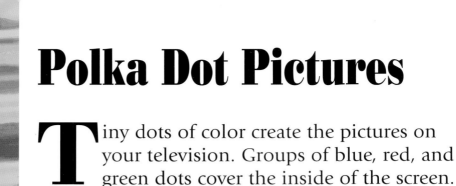

Television uses the primary colors of light, not pigment, because the television sends out light.

The primary-colored light is projected from the back of the television. It travels through a filter and lands on the screen.

The light appears as dots on the screen. The dots make up the picture.

Tiny dots of color also create the color pictures and photographs in books. These dots are drawn with the primary pigment colors and black. Use a magnifying glass to look at a picture in this book. You will see small groups of colored dots.

A famous group of artists called the Impressionists painted pictures using thousands of tiny dots of color. A French artist named Georges Seurat painted this picture.

Activity

Painting with Dots

You can make your own painting if you use dots of color. It will work best using a thin brush. Make the dots very small and close together. Combine different colored dots to make a picture.

From a distance, the dots blend together to make large areas of color.

Seeing Light and Color

Our eyes allow us to see light and color. Light enters the eye through an opening called the **pupil**. The pupil adjusts the amount of light coming into the eye. The pupil opens wide to let in as much light as possible when it is dark. In bright light, the pupil shrinks to a tiny hole. This allows only a small amount of light to enter. Too much light can damage the eye.

The pupil of a cat's eye opens wide in dim light and closes to a slit in bright sunlight.

A tiny lens directs light to the **retina** at the back of the eye. The retina detects the brightness and color of light. It contains cells called rods and cones. The rods tell how bright the light is. The cones detect the colors. Both the rods and cones send information to the brain through the **optic nerve**.

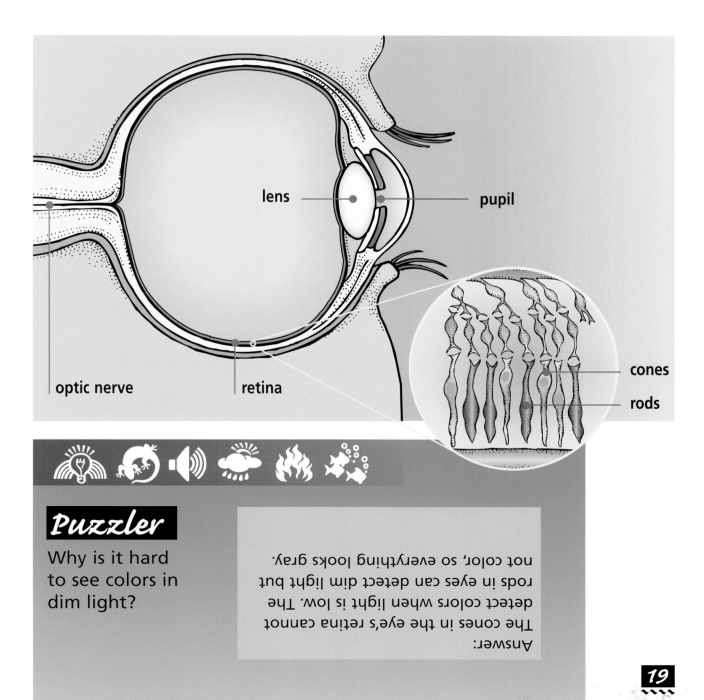

lens

pupil

optic nerve

retina

cones

rods

Puzzler

Why is it hard to see colors in dim light?

Answer:
The cones in the eye's retina cannot detect colors when light is low. The rods in eyes can detect dim light but not color, so everything looks gray.

Red and Green Cannot Be Seen

Some people cannot see colors well. These people are said to be **color vision deficient**. They have a hard time telling certain colors apart. Many color vision deficient people confuse reds and greens. This can cause problems when crossing streets with traffic lights. More boys and men are color vision deficient than girls and women. People who cannot see any colors at all are **color-blind**. They see the world in shades of gray.

People with color vision deficiency need to remember the order in which the colors appear on traffic lights. This way, they know when the light is green, and they can cross the street.

Some animals are color-blind. Dogs, horses, rabbits, and cows can see only shades of black, white, and gray. Many other animals can see color. Animals that do have good color vision include reptiles, birds, butterflies, bees, monkeys, and many fish.

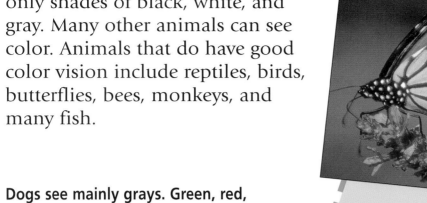

Dogs see mainly grays. Green, red, yellow, and orange all look the same to a dog.

Activity

Test for Color Vision Deficiency

Look at the picture. Can you see a hidden figure? It is made up of yellow and green dots. People who are color vision deficient cannot see it.

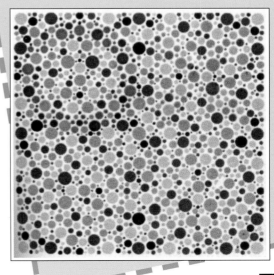

Plants and Light

Without sunlight, plants cannot grow. Plants are the basic source of food on Earth. Animals eat either plants or other creatures that eat plants. Plants also produce the oxygen we breathe.

Plants take in sunlight to grow. The plants absorb the light, which helps them make new leaves. The plants release oxygen into the air. They continue to absorb sunlight and to grow.

The green pigment in plant leaves is called **chlorophyll**. It absorbs the light plants use to make food and oxygen. Chlorophyll absorbs red, violet, and blue light. It reflects green light. This is why leaves look green.

In autumn, chlorophyll breaks down. It can no longer make the leaves green. This allows other pigments in the leaves to come through. We see them as the autumn colors of red, orange, gold, and brown.

Puzzler

Do leaves continue to make food from sunlight in autumn?

Answer: No, they need the green pigment chlorophyll to make food. Chlorophyll is no longer active in the leaves during the autumn.

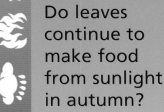

As days get shorter, there are fewer hours of sunlight. Leaves do not absorb enough light to stay green. The chlorophyll breaks down, and the many colors of fall appear.

Hiding in Color

Animals often take on the same colors and patterns as the world around them. This **camouflage** helps them blend into the background. It hides them from enemies.

Fawns
are especially well camouflaged when they are young. Their white spots help them disappear into the forest floor when they lie down.

Mother Birds
are often dull shades of brown or gray. They may also have speckles or small dots. These marks help them blend into the trees or ground where their nests are hidden. Eggs are often camouflaged by speckles or spots, too.

Walking Sticks
take on the shape and color of a stick or leaf. This helps them disappear from view while sitting on a bush.

Activity

Make Camouflage Pictures
Look through magazines to find pictures of animals that use camouflage. Ask permission to cut out the animal pictures. Paste the pictures on paper. Then paint a background in which they can hide.

Snowshoe Hares
change color when their surroundings change. They are white to match the snow in winter and brown to match the ground in summer.

Tigers and Leopards
have stripes or spots that help them hide while hunting. If they blend into the surroundings, it is easier for them to catch prey.

Focus on Photographers

Photographers use light and color to create pictures. They often specialize in black-and-white or color **photography**. Some photographers take pictures of wildlife, street scenes, landscapes, or news events. Others take wedding, sports, or school pictures.

Sometimes photographers shoot many rolls of film to get one really great picture.

If you want to become a professional photographer, you can take college or university classes in photography. You can also learn to be a photographer by becoming an **apprentice**. An apprentice works with and learns from a professional photographer.

Photographers often develop and print pictures in a darkroom. Only red light can be on in the room, or the pictures will be destroyed.

Warning Colors

Colors warn us about danger. Colors that give warnings are usually bright and easy to see. Traffic lights and traffic signs are red, yellow, and green — bright colors that are easily seen. Many emergency vehicles also have bright colors.

Poisonous animals are often brightly colored. Their colors are a warning to other animals that might eat them. Some harmless animals have colors and patterns that make them look like poisonous animals. This is called **mimicry**. Mimicry helps protect harmless animals from their enemies.

The poison dart frog and the coral snake use color to let everyone know that they are dangerous.

It is important to recognize warning colors and be aware of what they mean. Here are some hints that will help keep you and other people safe:

1. Always obey traffic signals. They keep people safe only if everyone follows the rules.

2. Stay away from places that have color warnings posted. The warnings may be red flags, yellow tape, or brightly colored signs.

3. Watch for the flashing colored lights of emergency vehicles. Police cars, ambulances, and fire trucks must move quickly. If you are crossing the street, get to the sidewalk as fast as you safely can.

Color Safari

Take an indoor safari to spot a wild and wacky bunch of animals. Look at this colorful picture. It contains animals wearing colors you might not find in nature. Their unusual colors are helping them hide in the crowd. Can you find all of the animals listed on the next page?

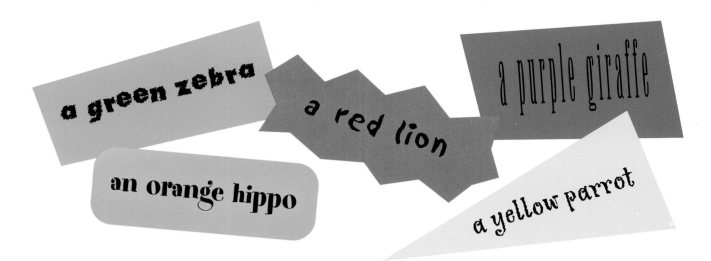

a green zebra

a purple giraffe

a red lion

an orange hippo

a yellow parrot

Glossary

absorbs: swallows up or takes in.

apprentice: a person who learns from a more experienced person.

camouflage: color, shape, or pattern that blends into the environment.

chlorophyll: green pigment in plant leaves that absorbs sunlight.

color-blind: unable to see colors.

color vision deficient: unable to tell the difference between certain colors.

mimicry: resembling another animal as a form of protection.

opaque: blocking light.

optic nerve: nerve that sends messages about light and color from the eyes to the brain.

oxygen: a gas people and most animals must breathe to stay alive.

photography: process of making pictures by exposing a film to light.

pigments: substances in objects that reflect colors.

primary colors: the three colors of light (red, blue, green) and of pigments (red, blue, yellow) from which all other colors can be mixed.

prism: a solid, flat-sided piece of glass that bends light.

pupil: a circular opening at the front of the eye that lets in light.

reflect: bounce off.

refraction: the bending of light.

retina: an area at the back of the eye where rods and cones detect the brightness and color of light.

transparent: allowing light to shine through.

Index

absorb 8, 15, 22, 23
animals 5, 10, 21, 22, 24, 25, 28, 30
apprentice 27

birds 21, 24

camouflage 24, 25
chlorophyll 23
color-blind 20, 21

color vision deficient 20, 21
cones 19
cyan 8

magenta 8
mimicry 28

opaque 11
optic nerve 19
oxygen 5, 22, 23

painting 17
photography 26, 27
pigment 14, 15, 16, 17, 23
plants 5, 22
primary colors 8, 9, 14, 16
prism 12, 13
pupil 18, 19

reflect 13, 15, 23
refraction 12
retina 19
rods 19

sunlight 8, 12, 13, 18, 22, 23

television 4, 16
transparent 8

Web Sites

www.brainpop.com/rainbow/

www.opticalres.com/kidoptx.html

amazing-space.stsci.edu/light

www.yorku.ca/eye/funthing.htm

Some web sites stay current longer than others. For further web sites, use your search engines to locate the following topics: *color, light, pigments, primary colors, prism,* and *rainbow.*

DATE DUE

HELLERTOWN LIBRARY